The Battle Between Emotion v. Logic

A Short Guide to Making Better Decisions
by Elevating Your Emotional Intelligence

By Dr. Jeffrey Donner

ISBN: 978-1-7320143-5-0

FREE GIFT FOR MY READERS

Watch the Free Webinar and learn the practical techniques to:

- Recognize your emotional state
- Control impulsive reactions
- Tai Chi Meditative Techniques
- Improved Sleeping
- How to combat stress
- Take back control in your life

WATCH NOW:
https://www.livingemotionalintelligence.com/webinar/

Table of Contents

Introduction

The battle has raged ever since man began standing upright. No matter how technologically advanced we become, the question remains. What controls us?

Is it our logic and our deductive/inductive reasoning, or is it our emotions, and our desires and impulsive reactions? You've been you for some time, so what is your conclusion to this dilemma? What do you think?

There is no question that both systems play a part, a role in our behavioral reactions. We want to believe we are logical, rational beings.

Logic is defined by Webster in this fashion: "A science that deals with the principles and criteria of validity of inference and demonstration: the science of the formal principles of reasoning." Inference is defined as: "the act of passing from one proposition, statement, or judgment considered as true to another whose truth is believed to follow from that of the former." (Also Webster). So first of all, logic is scientific, finding a truth and acting on it. But the key word in that definition is finding a judgment ***considered*** to be true.

Look around my friends, what I consider to be true, might not be so for you. Just watch the news, are the republicans and democrats on the same page regarding what is true and what isn't?

Why is there such variation? There is an answer! Read on.

CHAPTER 1

The Two Systems that Control Us!

Heart vs. Brain: The Battle for Control

"Your mind tells you what is smart and then your heart (and body) tells you what you're going to do!" –Khalifa

"Sometimes the heart should follow the mind, but sometimes the heart should tell the mind to stop interfering." –Unknown

You are in a store shopping for clothes- In your perusing of the different styles, you notice a blouse/or shirt that catches you eye. You weren't shopping for blouses, but this particular one is everything you like. You walk over to look further and it is your size. But you really don't need another blouse. When you look, the price of the blouse is expensive. You start putting it back, but then you think "I rarely buy things for myself!"

So, the question becomes – **Do you buy the blouse/shirt or not?**

Of course, this type of decision happens many times in the course of a year. It happens in regards to small things and in regards to big items. We often have trouble making decisions, even simple ones (where would you like to go out to eat?)

Some of us like to believe that we make decisions ***intellectually***, but the truth is when it comes to decision making...our ***emotions*** play a bigger role than we think.

Let me ask you a few questions?

- Have you ever let a smooth-talking salesperson talk you into making a large purchase that you regretted shortly thereafter?

- Have you used harsh words in an argument that you wish you never had done?

- Have you stayed in a relationship that you knew wasn't working or that was unhealthy because you were in denial?

- Have you ended a relationship because you over-reacted to something the other person said?

- Have you gotten into a lot of debt by making frivolous purchases?

If you answered **"YES"** to any of these questions, then your emotions might be calling the shots (don't be discouraged- they usually do!)

The fact is, whether we like it or not, we are guided and controlled by two systems: Logical (or Illogical) Intelligence and Emotion (***HEART VS. BRAIN***). We like to think that our intelligence guides our actions, but in truth our emotions probably play a bigger role in the things we do, than we would like to admit.

It's a tricky balance in us humans, we like to think of ourselves as logical, reasonable and in control. Unfortunately, if you're being honest, the opposite is often the case. Our emotions spike, sometimes very quickly. We get insulted, defensive and irritated, quicker than we would like. Our pride is a delicate thing, it can be easily injured. If you don't believe that your emotional system is the driving force in your activities, look with an *"ice-cold eye"* at T.V. commercials. They pander to your emotions, much more than they do your logic. You are shown a pretty or handsome face and told how wonderful life is if you buy this car. They even have cute bears, telling you how great their toilet paper is! Yes, they give you some logical reasons, but the crux of the commercial targets your emotional reaction.

Sure, there are days (weeks even) when we feel *"on top of the world"*. We feel good, we look good (this part degenerates over time), we have abundant energy, life is good. But then there are days that don't go so well. We screw up at work, or with friends or relatives, we do stupid things, we're human. (riding high in April, shot down in May) *"Some days you eat the bear, and some days the bear eats you!"* A friend once told me that some days he felt like he was standing on the beach, and he couldn't hit the ocean. We say and do impulsive things (look back and think "that was stupid").

This balance is continual and constantly changing. Some days I'm strong, and some days temptation and desires control me, and I give into bad habits. And after those "bad" days, my friendly companion *guilt*, pays me a visit. And I vow to do better, make a better plan, be stronger, stick with the plan, but…….. how long does that last? (maybe a week or two- if I'm lucky!). So, I vow again… and the beat goes on!

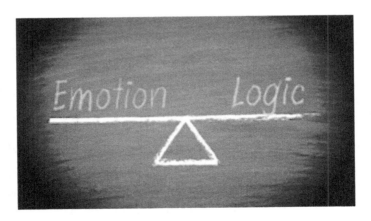

 I don't mean to make you feel discouraged, but we are people. This is our challenge, to improve, to hold the balance between intelligence and emotions, to lessen our worries, feel proud of ourselves. We are in a constant war between desires and our rationality. (By the way, if you can't relate to this, you're either in denial, or you're an alien).

I have driven by bakeries and heard some cookies calling my name, and have had to fight to keep driving.

We are rarely blessed with true balance. I'm sure you've known very bright people who are emotional children, and sweet people, who are not that sharp. Some people could call the person who has achieved balance, as someone who has common sense (I always thought it should be called uncommon sense, as few of us have it). But it's not hard to look over our lives and list all the stupid things we have done. I could write pages, so could you! Now, excluding drugs and alcohol (for when you mix these chemicals into the picture, our stupidity index rises dramatically), we all say and do many foolish things (with alarming frequency). I have worked with many people struggling with chemicals or other addictions. When they look over their lives, many of the worst things they have done is related to these addictions. But in truth, we are all pretty dopey.

Sometimes when we talk, before our sentences are finished, we already know we shouldn't be saying these things. And when we're angry look out, the kitchen sink is thrown in (we bring up issues and say things we really don't mean or throw out those trump cards we've been hanging onto for very long periods of time).

I used to say there were two rules in dealing with friends and relatives:

✓ Rule #1- Always keep your mouth closed

✓ Rule #2- Never, ever, forget rule #1.

Believe me I have failed at this rule many times over my life. And every time, I've paid the price. Our mouths lead us into many bad places (maybe that's why animals don't talk- people used to say your mouth gets your nose in trouble). I once knew of an attorney who had a large stuffed fish hanging on the back wall behind his desk. A friend asked him if he was a fisherman and he responded "no". So "why do you have the fish hanging behind your desk?" "Read the inscription" replied the attorney. The man walked up to the stuffed animal and it read "I wouldn't have gotten caught either, if I would have kept my mouth shut".

All this aside, our intelligence or rationality is frequently guided, or undermined, by our emotions. We often buy things because we want them (they make us feel good), not always because we need them. We are sometimes (or often) impulsive, reacting before we think. We fall prey to good salesmen or fancy advertising, and then realize we've been duped.

Believe it or not, our emotions fuel our actions. Without emotional input we evaluate, but don't do anything.

It's been suggested that 80% of all decision-making is emotion, and only 20% is logic.

So, one of the goals of life is to balance your emotions and your logic. Not let either rule the day (much easier said than done). You will learn more of this when you watch the Webinar attached to this small book.

CHAPTER 2

Emotional Leaking and the 5 Monsters of Unhealthy Emotions

Is your emotional roof leaking? What does that really mean?

Well, did you ever go into a restaurant and see all the happy people and wonder, "How come my family and I, are not as happy as them?" Well that's one of life's great illusions my friends. When we see other people, we really don't know what's going on inside of their house. Somebody once said, "you can't tell if the roof is leaking until you go inside the house."

This short book is about going inside, both in our own emotional house, and peeking through the windows of others. This book is the first step on an emotional journey to fix the roof.

But there are five monsters that undermine our happiness. In my writings I have called them *"under-emotions."* When pressures and stress take control of us we lose our happiness and replace it with these under-emotions. So what are these five monsters of our emotional chaos?

What to look for in ourselves and others...
The five under-emotions

Here are hints about what to look for in ourselves and others to tell whether their emotional roof is leaking. Now remember you're going to try and see these things in others, god-forbid you see them in yourself. "I mean, I'm not like this!"

Monster #1
Under Emotion #1
Rigidity

We have all known rigid people- some will call them **"closed minded,"** and that they are. Rigid people show an inability to change or adapt to circumstance. When we are rigid, we block off our mental processes- blocking off routes to solve problems. Rigid thinkers are not creative. They stick obsessively to rules (mistaken beliefs they think are rules) even in the face of stupidity (in problem solving terms they continue to try and stuff the round block into the square hole).

There is only one way of doing things- "It's either my way or the highway." Rigid people are actually scared of change. Rigid people always refer to the past. "This is the way it's supposed to be!" "No I've tried this before (20 years) and it didn't work"

The good news is that mental flexibility can be learned, **if you want to learn it.** It's not an easy process because it involves embracing your mistakes and not rejecting other solutions quickly. And you have to stay away from absolutes. You have to learn how to think outside the emotional box.

Einstein said "The mind that opens up to new ideas, will never return to its original size"

An offshoot of rigidness is **stubbornness**. In many ways they are the same under emotion. "refuse to move from this spot or accept any change." Stubborn people have difficulty changing their mental sets. They cannot understand things from somebody else's point of view. They stubbornly adhere to what they "think" is truth, or what they want to believe is truth.

John Maynard Keys said "The difficulty lies not in the new ideas, but escaping from the old ones"

Monster #2
Under emotion #2
Self-Defeating Patterns or Behaviors

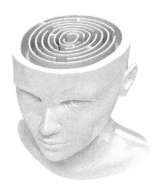

The second monster, or under emotion to look for in others (and ourselves) are **Self-defeating cycles-** We are very patterned individuals. A simple test: do you put your socks on before your pants, or vice versa? Whichever it is, try for a few days doing it the opposite way. It's not as easy as it sounds. Another example: some people put one sock on then the shoe on that foot. Other people put both socks on and then their shoes. Which pattern do you do? Try the other pattern.

So, you see our patterns shape our lives. Well the two I mentioned are simple patterns. They really don't impact our lives. But there are other patterns that have tremendous influence.

Some negative emotional patterns are: holding grudges; quickly insulting others; quick emotional reactions (always feeling hurt); giving others the silent treatment when we're angry; repetitive emotional conflicts; denying intimacy; and, on and on Infinitum.

Ross Perot once commented "The Key to hunting, is not shooting yourself in the foot"

So what patterns that you have (figuratively) "shoots yourself in the foot" and what are your positive patterns (i.e. going to the gym, paying bills on time, not building up too much debt, staying close to loved ones, not overreacting to trivialities).

What negative patterns can you observe in others? Watch your significant other or your co-workers. What do they regularly do that makes you want to scratch your head in disbelief? You say to yourself "why do they do that?"

Some patterns are completely unconscious (i.e. twirling your hair, bouncing your foot when anxious, biting your lip, picking at yourself, starting every sentence with "so"). In poker, these are called *"tells."* There are unconscious emotional patterns as well (i.e. calling yourself stupid, ruminating over minor mistakes, lying about silly things).

Actually, there is an interesting statistic about lying. It seems as though, even though we believe that we can spot liars, in fact, we are not very good at it.

Only 53% of the time do we actually spot a liar.

So, it's like a coin flip.

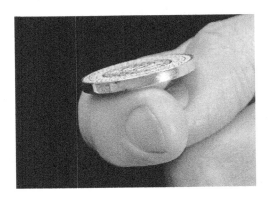

There are some common tells that are often true (often is a key word- or substitute- not always-when evaluating certain things about people: the context of the situation needs to be taken into account). One of the more valid and reliable tells is the inconsistency of behavior (not being able to keep their story straight). Another one is if a person's emotions are inappropriate for the situation (major over or under reactions, or if they laugh when they shouldn't be). People who say one thing and do another is a significant behavioral tell that you need to take special consideration with.

The old Irish saying is "Fool me once, shame on you, fool me twice, shame on me!"

Monster #3
Under Emotion #3
Drama

The next area to look for which might tell you that other's "emotional roof" is leaking, is Drama. It is also called the "Chicken Little – the sky is falling syndrome." Some people live off the drama of situations. Some people love to spread rumors and tell others about somebody's troubles. Drama is an avoidance and a negative problem-solving strategy (a very common and dangerous under emotion- It is common because social media lives on it, and many of us live on social media- it is a very seductive under emotion). It is making your feelings someone else's responsibility.

Facebook addiction, phone addiction, always watching heart wrenching TV dramas, fuels our dramatic side (like gas on a fire). Gossiping is a big issue in this area. You know people who are always telling you bad news about others. "Did you hear that she did this?" Well some of this is normal curiosity, and we all gossip to a point. But many of us cross that line. The trouble with gossip is that often the rumors we spread, are not true. But some of us live on dirt, feel comfortable in it, and relish playing in it- our pockets and shoes are filled with emotional dirt ("I love to hear about other's dirty laundry")

Did you know that there are 1030 synonyms for the word gossip (ex. Chatter, rumor, babble, etc.)? It's been estimated that 60-80% of all conversation is gossip. A very powerful under emotion.

Well of course, everyone has engaged in office gossip. Not only is it seductive (hard to avoid) but it's fun. Let's admit it. Gossip has both positive and negative characteristics. On the positive side we can bond over it- (a way of determining friends and building social bonds) and in the negative, it can be a form of bullying (relational aggression). We all detest cyberbullies- but people get off on it. When you have a colleague and you both detest a fellow worker, there is enjoyment in discussing and relishing in their weaknesses (somehow it validates us and makes us feel stronger). "I might have problems, but their problems are worse!"

Interestingly, the more competitive a person is, the more they might tend to gossip. Men and woman tend to gossip about different things (woman about social things and appearance; men about achievement and macho things). Think about television and celebrity stuff. It's mostly gossip and innuendo. The Kardashian's built a fortune on gossip, and drama. Most reality shows thrive on it.

So, watch for the gossipers. The people who gossip the most are telling you about their emotional roof (some don't have small leaks, but Niagara Falls). We can forgive adolescents for their gossip obsession, but adults are a different story. I once ran a school for emotionally disturbed children and adolescents. I would go into the teacher's cafeteria to have lunch. I eventually stopped the practice, because all I heard was gossip. This teacher, this child, this family, on and on. And yet if you ask, most people deny they gossip or spread rumors. And yes, gossiping is a way of spreading rumors. "Did you hear what John did, it's shameful."

Monster #4
Under emotion #4
Denial

People often ask therapists about Happiness. How do I become happier? Although this might sound counter-intuitive, one of the ways to increase personal happiness is to face what some would call "brutal facts" about ourselves and others. Some also call it "inconvenient truths." There is a reality out there, that begs to differ with some of your beliefs and fears! Some people will avoid going to a doctor, but whatever is troubling them, already exists! Avoiding it only makes it more chronic.

Denial is a self-protective defense mechanism that we use to shelter us from our fears, our mistakes, and our truths about ourselves and others. And make no mistake, we deny as much about our loved ones, as we do about ourselves.

I have never met a parent who hasn't told me how bright their children are.

I had a mentor that once told me that we live in a room with translucent black curtains covering the window. Every once in a while, a curtain rises and a little more light gets in. And sometimes all the curtains rise, and we actually see the truth. Some of us at this time, hurry to close the curtains, for the light of truth hurts our eyes. It has been referred to as an "oh shit" moment.

Truth can cause us many problems. Just think of addiction. Having worked with many addicts, their rationalization systems are firmly entrenched in their addictive behavior patterns ("I actually drive better when I'm drunk")

In fact, all denial is self-sabotaging!

This is the pattern:

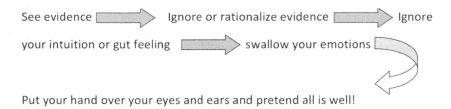

See evidence ⟶ Ignore or rationalize evidence ⟶ Ignore your intuition or gut feeling ⟶ swallow your emotions

Put your hand over your eyes and ears and pretend all is well!

Put your hand over your eyes and ears and pretend all is well!

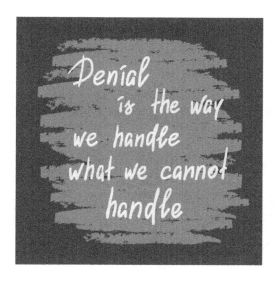

The old comedian, Lenny Bruce once joked. "If you're naked on top of another woman and your wife walks in, deny it"

And denial often leads to this next monster—blaming others!

Monster #5
Under Emotion #5
Projection of blame

This is last of the monsters that will tell you that either you, or the other person, has a leaky emotional roof, is *projection of blame.*

When my children were young we used to have someone, who lived in our house called "Not Me". Well *Not Me* did a lot of stuff. But children are just that, children. It's different when an adult claims "Not Me"

Carl Jung said "The most dangerous psychological mistake is the projection of the shadow onto others, this is the root of almost all conflicts"

I remember once, during a therapy session with an adolescent (about 14) sitting with her mother. The adolescent was failing everything in school, and the mother accused her of having an attitude problem. With a nastiness of tone, the adolescent said "Mother, it's not me with the attitude problem, it's you". And then, for the next twenty minutes, the mother attempted to defend herself, denying that she had a problem. Now look how beautiful that manipulation is. The adolescent didn't have to answer for her issues but shifted the onus onto the mother.

This example is a typical manipulation, often used by people when they have no defense. In courts, it's been called "Plan B". If you can't defend your client, blame somebody else, create doubt. (most children are interns for law school- and the more we as parents fall for and give into this denial under-emotion, the more we teach our children the usefulness of Denial)

Anger and irresponsibly are two of our most frequent emotional projections onto others. When we're being accused of something in an argument, we often bring up the faults of the other person "Yeah but you did this or that." Children often blame siblings for things they forgot to do or should have done, or mistakes that were made. Children are very transparent in their projections, but adults are much more sophisticated and manipulative.

We will often engage others in our projection. If you feel wronged, you come home from work and tell your significant others about how horrible you were treated. Your significant other will frequently agree and validate your position. But if he or she doesn't give you enough validation, you can always turn to a tried and true place for validation (usually one of your parents). Then you can call a best friend, to tell him/her about the situation, and get more validation for your position.

What is a true friend? A true friend tells you the truth! Somebody once said "Truth is like surgery, it hurts, then it cures"

You know the expression "The truth hurts", but the next line is "but the lies kill you"

On an off note, Narcissists are experts at shifting blame- they are specialists in this field. It's actually called **blame shifting.** (Just as a side note- there are a few clear signs of narcissism—what I say is the only thing that matters in our conversation- everything is always about me, rules are meant for others, not me; I'm right and you're wrong, and that never changes. So, any problems between us has to be your fault.)

The other thing that people do to avoid responsibility is to play the victim "Yes I'm always wrong and you're always right—I'm a horrible parent/person".

Then there is the last type of blame. It's been called the last resort of projection- the *stink bomb approach* (Mackenzie). Throwing an unfounded accusation at you (i.e. you've never loved me). Again, it's purpose is to put the other person on the defensive and have them have to defend themselves.

But to be honest, there is also an insidious type of blame – it is when we only blame ourselves. You get ignored by your boss and spend the day trying to figure what you've done wrong, when in actuality it probably had nothing to do with you. There is a *"9 out of 10"* rule in psychology. That is when you blame yourself for something, 9 out of 10 times it probably had nothing to do with you"

So these are a few "tells" ways you can look into someone else's house to see if the roof is leaking (there are obviously more- but these are major ones). So let's summarize the 5 Monsters of unhealthy under-emotions:

Rigidity:

> *"Free yourself from the rigid conduct of tradition and open yourself to the new forms of probability"– Hans Bende*

Denial:

> *"Denial ain't just a river in Egypt"– Mark Twain*

Gossip and Drama:

> *"The only time people dislike gossip is when you gossip about them" – Will Rodgers*

Self-Defeat

> *"Many forms of self-defeating behavior are unseen and un-conscious, which is why their existence is denied" – Vernon Howard*

Blaming Others:

"You can make mistakes, but you aren't a failure until you start blaming others for your mistakes" – John Wooden

CHAPTER 3

An Introduction to Emotional Intelligence and a Tiny Test

What Is Emotional Intelligence and What It Is NOT?

You may not know the term, but "Cognitive Intelligence" is the ability to solve problems. (I don't mean math, I mean everyday ongoing issues we have) "Should I do this? How should I approach this situation?" Etc. etc. Even simple problems like- what are we having for supper, requires problem solving. The legendary detective Sherlock Holmes and his ability to deduce things from clues is a good example of a person with a high level of cognitive intelligence. Other examples are: Mr. Spock on Star Trek- Sheldon on The Big Bang Theory. But emotional intelligence (although it does take in some cognitive characteristics) is quite different.

What is Emotional Intelligence?

Emotional Intelligence is the ability to understand your own emotional states (and how to react and act with them), and the ability to read and understand the emotional states of others (and how to act and react to them- some of this part involves deductive reasoning). In many ways, it is much more complicated than problem solving. Why more complicated (I hear you cry), because our emotions distort our cognition. "I don't like this guy, so whatever he says or does must be stupid, and wrong", "My child? my child wouldn't lie to me!" People who don't believe their loved ones lie, are lying to themselves! Look at relationships, with those you love.

You know one of the biggest problems in marital therapy is the other person believing they can read the mind and intentions of their spouse. "I know what he said, but what he really means is......" And think about Christmas and Birthdays. This person whom you love, your best friend and soul mate. How often does he/she give you a present you really want? (Now come on, leaving hints is not included, like leaving open magazines with what you want circled with a marker!). So, if it's difficult with those we love, how can we evaluate those we don't love, but only work with, or are friends to. How difficult is it to read them? (for those of us who have been stabbed in the back by a good friend).

"I love him/her to death!" I don't like that comment. Because, it's usually followed by a "but.........." And some sort of disparaging remark. "I love him to death but he's a jerk". (see I didn't curse).

So, the statement "I love him/her to death" is only a way of relieving my guilt about what I'm going to say after it.

First a Tiny Test... The "Who is Me Test"

Obviously, the answers are very personal. I will give you a sense on how to score and what it means, but it isn't standardized and it should be understood with this grain of salt. Try to be as honest as you can (honesty is a tough concept for us as humans. We easily will distort or exaggerate situations. So, are we being honest?") You might want to rate your significant other and then let him/her rate themselves (and you) and see what the difference is. A major difference between your rating of yourself and the rating of another, could signify a major roof leak (OMG there is a flood on the floor!).

So let's begin:

All of the questions will be presented with this kind of rating

Strongly Agree (5) - Agree Somewhat (4) - Neutral (3) - Slightly Disagree (2) - Strongly Disagree (1)

General State of Self

Strongly Agree (5) - Agree Somewhat (4) - Neutral (3) - Slightly Disagree (2) - Strongly Disagree (1)

☐ I am generally a happy person

☐ There is not much about myself I would like to improve

(A ten in this section is unreasonable- we usually have things we want to improve- an 8 or a 9 is a good score—Anything under an 8 could identify some leaks in your emotional ceiling.)

Professional Life

Strongly Agree (5) - Agree Somewhat (4) - Neutral (3) - Slightly Disagree (2) - Strongly Disagree (1)

☐ I am contented with my professional status and position

☐ I know how to avoid power struggles at work

☐ My emotions do not get in my way at work

☐ I do not overreact to situations at work

☐ I believe I can read and understand the emotions of my co-workers

☐ I do not carry my emotions home from work

☐ I have a good work-life balance

(Hopefully the answer to the first question is a 5- or a 4 at best. Anything less than a 20 on questions 2-3-4-5 is going to identify a leaky roof- and anything less than a 4 on the last question is cause for concern)

Family Life

Strongly Agree (5) - Agree Somewhat (4) - Neutral (3) - Slightly Disagree (2) - Strongly Disagree (1)

☐ I am tuned in to the emotions of my family members

☐ I do not overreact to family issues

☐ I (figuratively) do not feel like smacking my family members (on a regular basis)

☐ I know how to avoid power struggles with my spouse and my children

☐ I feel I communicate well with all of my family members

☐ There are no family relationships I need to improve

Self-Understanding

Strongly Agree (5) - Agree Somewhat (4) - Neutral (3) - Slightly Disagree (2) - Strongly Disagree (1)

☐ I know my emotional triggers (what makes me angry-guilty-sad)

☐ I rarely use excuses to justify my behavior

☐ I am not impulsive in my reactions (this includes financial and emotional)

☐ I know how to forgive myself and others

☐ I know how to duck others comments (avoid nasty comments of others)

☐ I do not carry my emotions around with me (let things bother me for long periods of time)

☐ I do not take my anxiety or other emotions out on my body

(I hope you rate 5 on the first question. A five on the second, will mean denial has creeped in, and a 5 on the third is an "Are you serious?" The fourth question is very important. Forgiveness of yourself and others is one of the ways to reduce underlying anger. The answer to question 6 is also important-if you dwell or ruminate on problems or mistakes, there is clearly a leak that can become toxic if not fixed. If you get a five on the last question in this section, denial is also involved. Try to identify the body system that you take anxiety and stress out on)

Understanding of Others

Strongly Agree (5) - Agree Somewhat (4) - Neutral (3) - Slightly Disagree (2) - Strongly Disagree (1)

☐ I believe I can read others well (not just people I'm familiar with, but even people I do not know)

☐ I am usually not wrong when evaluating others

☐ I do not believe in first impressions

☐ I understand the politics of my workplace

☐ I am not intimidated by others who are professionally my superiors

☐ I believe I can read faces

(Often a high score on question 1 is again a denial issue. And if you get a five on #2 you better check your roof. Question 3 is an interesting one, because we are often greatly influenced by first impression (that's why psychopaths are so successful in their business). Number 4 is tricky because office politics can be like walking in a land mine. Especially entering a new position. Office politics can embroil you in drama you never wished upon. Most people don't consider the importance of question 6)

Relaxation

Strongly Agree (5) - Agree Somewhat (4) - Neutral (3) - Slightly Disagree (2) - Strongly Disagree (1)

☐ I know how to soothe myself when I am upset

☐ I regularly practice meditation

☐ I regularly practice relaxation

☐ I have a hobby I really love

☐ I know how to disengage from the world of work

(I hope you give yourself a high score on the first and the last questions in this section. I hope the way you soothe yourself doesn't include chemicals "Oh yeah, I just have 4 or 5 beers" The answer to question 4 is really important. Everyone needs something they can look forward to.)

Relationships

Strongly Agree (5) - Agree Somewhat (4) - Neutral (3) - Slightly Disagree (2) - Strongly Disagree (1)

☐ I am generally successful in choosing relationships

☐ I have a lot of personal support

☐ I know how to trust others

☐ I believe others trust me

☐ I am not harboring any serious hurts or angers about people

☐ I know how to let the past go

(Because we don't usually read people well, many people choose poor relationships. Some of my clients have believed their wear a sign that attracts poor relationships. Nobody wears a sign, but if you do attract poor relationships it means you better figure out what you're missing in reading people.

I once ran a group for young woman who had relationship issues. They came up with a number of rules for dating- Rule #1- never date someone you met in a bar; Rule#2- never date someone who is not working (no matter what great excuse they use for it); Rule

#3- never date someone who lives with their mother; and, Rule #4 never date someone who is a Mets fan (a funny rule- but it takes courage and some level of masochism, to be a long term Mets fan)

Trust is a big issue in relationships. Are you a trustworthy person (No excuses). The past is the past, don't get stuck in it.)

Sleep

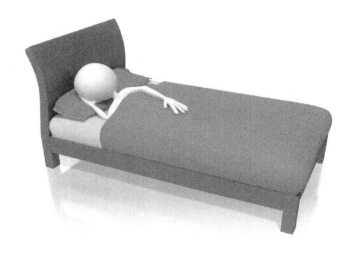

Strongly Agree (5) - Agree Somewhat (4) - Neutral (3) - Slightly Disagree (2) - Strongly Disagree (1)

☐ I sleep well

☐ It does not take me a long time to fall asleep

☐ I awake rested

☐ I am usually not tired during the day

☐ I do not have restless sleep

(Sleep is very important to functioning at efficient levels. Just ask a mother with an infant, or an adolescent who stays up late playing video. The answer to question 2 is important. Are you still dealing with problems that are interfering with your ability to rest?)

Coping Strategies

Strongly Agree (5) - Agree Somewhat (4) - Neutral (3) - Slightly Disagree (2) - Strongly Disagree (1)

- [ ] I can accurately anticipate situations

- [ ] I know how to set priorities

- [ ] I can easily find humor in life

- [ ] I pay attention to my feelings

- [ ] I evaluate my assumptions

- [ ] I actively work on my goals

- [ ] I do not overuse life strategies of avoidance

- [ ] I do not overuse chemicals to avoid.

(Humor is very important in life. Somebody once said hope does not solve problems, setting and achieving goals does.)

"When I let go of what I am, I become what I might be"

Lao Tzu

So this tiny "Who is Me" test is not all inclusive. In fact, I hope you learned a little about your emotional intelligence by taking this tiny test. It is only a brief evaluation and introduction to ourselves, and what we think about ourselves. There are obviously no right answers. But if you were honest with yourself- you can see both your strengths and weaknesses. You can see which areas might be leaking and which areas are solid. You can identify the leaks in your roof! (the first step in changing is identifying the problem)

Just remember, don't get down on yourself or your significant other if you saw things you weren't expecting. These things are fixable, with the right effort and the correct direction. And the probability is that improving your level of emotional intelligence is a very good place to start.

We all have areas we need to constantly monitor and improve. You know, we live in a very complex and changing world. There are many challenges for us to master as we grow. Every age, as we mature, has its own trials and tribulations. We have many stresses. But the key to stress isn't to avoid it (because that is virtually impossible). In fact, short term stress is very helpful, it motivates us to improve. The problem with stress is if it becomes long term. If it hangs over our head like a dark cloud that rarely leaves. Stress then becomes very toxic to us, and destructive to our system.

CHAPTER 4

Toxic Stress and the FFF Response

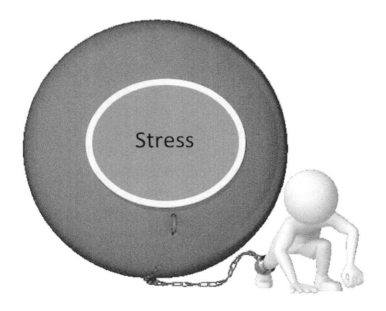

Stress this, stress that- but what actually is stress, and why do I have it? I don't want it, I want it to go away- now! I can feel stress- I can feel it in my muscles, in my head, in my neck. I also can think stress- feeling overwhelmed (I want to get in the car and leave). You can tell when others are under stress- they react like reptiles- want to bite your head off. You can tell when someone is stressed, just by the way they look at you- they either look beat up, or like they want to beat you up. So back to question: What is stress?

Well stress can be defined *"as a state of mental or emotional tension arising from an adverse or very demanding circumstance."* Your body actually believes it is under attack when you are stressed.

"I may look calm, but in my head, I've killed you three times"

"So you mean to tell me a stress ball is not something you throw at people when they stress you out"

> *"I miss me- the old me- the happy me- the laughing me- the gone me"* unknown

So it's dangerous stuff this stress- drains us of our happiness- drains us of our smile- drains us of our life. So therefore, it must be a disease-right? Meets all the criteria (hurts your body- you worry about it- makes you tired and cranky- it's even contagious- in fact it's especially contagious when I'm around certain people- maybe it's an allergy- I'm allergic to certain people. So when the Dr. asks me what I'm allergic to I will say: "penicillin, milk and uncle bob"—so why doesn't using hand sanitizer protect me from this thing (who can I write to and complain?). If I wear a mask, will I not get this stress stuff. Is it airborne?

I joke, but stress is much more insidious than many illnesses. Like anything else, a little stress is good for you (creates motivation)- but if you cross that invisible line- you enter the danger zone.

You see stress is very sticky- hard to get rid of it once you have it.

But there is good news- You can learn the skills to manage it. Now I don't mean the five monsters- I'll deny I have it- blame others for it- hide my head in the sand- drink myself silly- buy a new car. These avoidant strategies don't work- and I thought they would, but they don't.

Do you know that 32% of us identify that we're under extreme stress (web, MD)

77% of us believe that we have physical problems due to stress (fatigue- headaches- muscle problems)-

And, almost half of us believe that our stress is on the rise- And by the way- this disease reaches all ages- crosses all racial barriers- does not distinguish between men and woman. There is no vaccine for it!

The Fight or Flight Response

I'm sure you've heard of the *"fight and flight response"*. There is actually a third F- *freeze* (when we feel frozen in our response- frozen with anger, guilt, fear, worry, surprise etc. This is an emotional dysregulation). When we experience the 3 F response- there are many physiological reactions that accompany it. The 3 F system was downloaded into our genetic computer for a purpose. A short term reason. It was initially given to us to save our lives. It energizes our system to an optimal point to deal with danger. (example: blood is transferred to the muscles so we can react- you've heard of someone getting super human strength during a crisis). But, the bad news is that if the reaction continues to happen over and over (or if we're in and out of it many, many times during a day), it leads to a buildup of hormones leading to **Toxic stress.**

Toxic stress (stress that doesn't get resolved) has the following long-term effects:

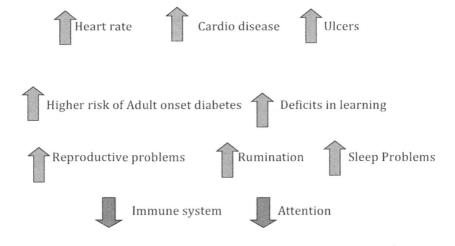

Living with high levels of toxic stress it's like waiting for your body and head to explode.

So, stress is a very deadly enemy to carry around. It's not a question of if it will get you, it's a question of when and how!

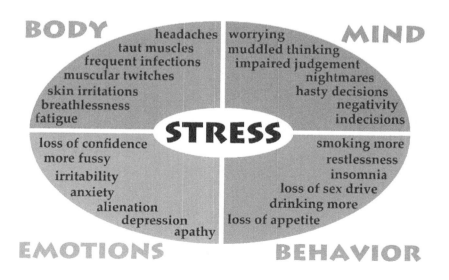

But I'd like you to take a minute of reflection. Take a few cleansing breathes, (breath in through your nose, and push your stomach out- hold for one beat, and out through your mouth, while pulling your stomach in.) Center yourself! (clear your mind)

I don't want any panic. Remember I said all this is fixable. Remember we cannot change the stress itself, but we can change how we react to it!

Now think—Am I where I want to be in life? Everything considered- How am I doing?

For all we know, we only live once. Am I happy with my situation and position?

A Tiny Insight into Your Brain's Amygdala

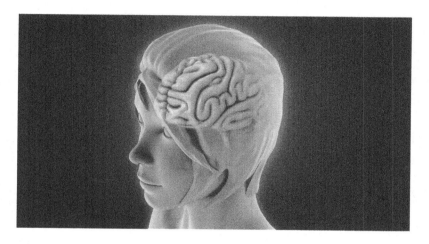

Let us go quickly into a brief bit of neurology (I promise it won't hurt....much) We spoke about the fight/flight/freeze response (**FFF**). Well, there is a small, almond like section of the brain that controls this response. It is called the Amygdala. Whenever our senses read something troubling in the environment, this little amygdala jumps into action and triggers the FFF response. Now often, this happens **completely unconscious** of our cognitive evaluation. It is an automated system. Our senses actually evaluate things and send the messages to the amygdala.

I told you about the two systems that guide us (emotions and logic), well there are two physiological systems that guide us as well. They are the **gas pedal system (the sympathetic reactive system)** and the **brake system (the parasympathetic system).**

The gas pedal system engages quickly before we know it-- from a message from the amygdala (the forward scout). The amygdala sends a message to the commander (hypothalamus).

The commander then contacts the gland guys to get into action (the adrenal and pituitary). The gland guys then produce adrenaline and cortisol.

Long term fight and flight reaction or toxic stress causes the internal organs to become depleted- and leads to **organ burnout.** So, we don't want to eliminate the gas pedal system, only to control it and learn how to activate the brake system. (by the way, besides the slowing of heart rate, the relaxation of muscles, the improvement in digestion, the brake system also controls sexual arousal- added side benefit)

But, have no fear, there is also something called **"Top down control"**. Top down control is our ability, our volitional control, our will power, to control our reactions (if we turn it on). Now, this doesn't mean avoidance of problems (which is quite detrimental to our stress level). But we have the ability to reappraise (redefine) our situation and thereby regulate our emotional responses (both prepare for stressful situations and learn how to initiate the brake system). So, rather than overreact, create drama, catastrophize (OMG- this is a stab in the heart), and lose sight of everything in an emotional hurricane, we can control FFF with our preparation and our thoughts. "Think (reappraise) twice before you react"

Top down control is a developmental process, dramatically strengthening throughout adolescence and adulthood. The prefrontal and frontal areas of the brain gain strength and learn to inhibit impulsivity and overreaction. So, top down control allows us to supersede initial reaction patterns, to ignore certain environmental irrelevancies and allow multitasking. It is the use of thought, to override reaction.

Reframing our initial negative or fearful thoughts, understanding and putting the situation into perspective and context, lessens the toxic nature of the stress. So, the development and practice of Top Down Control will reduce toxic stress. So, in general, we want to do **less**: avoidance, denial, distraction, rumination and less DRAMA! We want to do **more**: planning for stress, reformulating our thoughts, reappraising the situation, more proper labeling, more finding support and more problem solving. Patience is a big issue here.

Thoughts that Control or Modulate Emotional responses:

- It's not as Bad as I first thought
- This won't last forever
- This will be better soon
- The worst is over
- This is worth it
- These problems are normal
- How will I feel about this next week? Next Year?
- Will this still bother me in 5 years?
- What would I tell a friend to do in this situation?

Always look for the light at the end of the tunnel. Identify it (this will be over in ......). My pain is temporary. Unfortunately, some pain is not temporary, but there are strategies for that as well.

We've spoken of the battle between your emotions and your logic. In the **free Webinar**, (Escaping the Emotional Swamp) you will learn a series of questions that will help you determine the roots of a particular problem. When your emotional reaction brings you to the edge of catastrophe, these questions will help you reel yourself in. The questions will help you engage your logic.

CHAPTER 6

Tools to Give Your Brain a Break

How do I learn how to activate the brake system and incorporate top down control over my reactions?

Let me briefly summarize to put some things together. You are aware of the two systems that control our reactions (emotions and logic). These control how we make everyday decisions. You've learned how to begin identifying whether your roof is leaking (or for that matter- whether your significant others have seepage). You know the five monsters of the underemotions and how they limit our ability to adjust to an ever-changing world. You have a brief introduction to emotional intelligence- what it is and what it is not. You've learned about toxic stress and the terrible ongoing consequences of it. You learned about the two physiological systems that make up the autonomic nervous system (the pedal and the brake systems).

So now the question is: What do I do about all this? (I hear you cry)

Well emotional intelligence is really learning top down control. It is preparing for stress, understanding yourself and others, and not being blindsided either in work or at home.

Besides learning top down control, we also need to learn how to activate the brake system to undermine the petal system (if you never turn off the cruise control you will run head long into the car in front of you!).

So in this last chapter, I will outline some ways to activate the brake system.

Relaxation

There are many practical reasons to learn to conquer the relaxation task. It is something that we westerners don't do well. Yes, we take vacations, but learn and use a relaxation discipline- not usually. Don't have time for that. Got to squeeze every second of the day into something we consider productive. Then at night, we go unconscious- or have trouble falling sleeping.

Six Typical Symptoms of Burnout

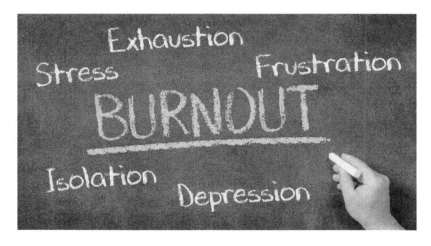

1. Irritability- general mistrust of other's intentions (a little paranoid)

2. No new ideas in past six months (brain on hold)

3. Lack of energy – physical and emotional (Just let me be)

4. Feelings of isolation and lack of support (identifying only one or two people you can trust)

5. Urge to get out of present job (the grass is always greener)

6. Gauge my success by focusing on quantity not quality.

Relaxation (consciously turning off cruise control and initiating the brake system) holds a number of physiological pluses that need to be recognized. It's funny how we will go to a gym and work out, take supplements, go on diets, but not take seriously the need to de-stress. So, what are the advantages:

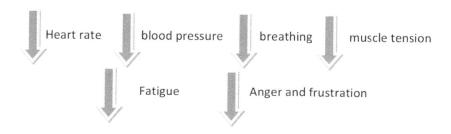

Reduce Toxic Stress and organ burn out

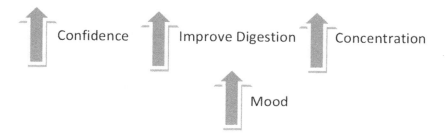

With all these benefits, one would have to wonder why we choose not to participate. Unless it's "When I die I want my jaw clenched," or "I enjoy grinding my teeth down."

There are actually many "roads" to get to the end result of relaxation or reducing toxic stress. There is: progressive muscle relaxation, visualization, reduction in breath per minute; Tai Chi; Meditation; and, Yoga. These are only a few of the exhaustive list, and I should point out that "Different Strokes for Different folks" applies. Some people are very comfortable with one approach, whereas others are comfortable with another. None of them is inherently superior to the others- they will all bring you to the promised land.

All will work……if……you……use……them.

IF is the key word here!

For thirty some years I played racquetball almost every morning. I often did my Tai Chi exercises before getting on the court. One of my partners would comment that he always knew when I had done Tai Chi before racquetball, for I concentrated much better. In my mind it appeared as though I could slow the ball down better. I felt more "in the zone".

An important approach to relaxation and stress reduction is called **Coherent Breathing**. It is a systematic approach to reducing your breath to five breaths a minute. It is combined with Qi Gong exercise (an ancient Chinese approach to exercise and breath control—Robert Peng is one of the many experts in the skill) to further the relaxation process. Although I will not go into detail here, I will refer you to the two major experts in the field: Dr. Richard Brown and Dr. Patricia Gerbarg. They have co-authored two groundbreaking books: **"The Healing Power of Breath"** and **"The Rhodiola Revolution."** The Dr's have extensive training experience in teaching the breath reduction. They run the Breath Body Mind Institute in New York. There is extensive research on the physiological and psychological impact of Coherent Breathing.

In western culture, we have developed a strange mindset. Everything is about more. Getting more- building my resume- getting home faster- more and more multitasking- sleeping less- working more- trying to squeeze more and more into the time we have. Our lives go by without us even knowing it. We sit in a room and listen to a lecture (that we wanted to hear) and our minds are more concerned with what we will do after the lecture. We clean the kitchen, and while we do it, we're thinking about our next task.

I once had a friend who hiked through the Grand Canyon. But while seeing these amazing sights, he commented that all he could think about was how he would tell everyone about what he saw. He couldn't enjoy the splendor of the moment.

So where have we gone wrong? How have we gotten into this Type A- hell on earth? The trouble is most of us don't realize the situation until we begin running out of time, then we look back and say "where has it all gone?" In truth, in the scheme of things, our life passes by quickly. The comment of "Take time to smell the roses," everyone agrees with, but few of us actually do. The only way to slow down time is to learn to stay in the present.

Everyone gives us Points today- an interesting advertising scheme that convinces us we are better with points. It reminds me of an old story:

The Garden Reading

Life was fun for Adam and Eve. They climbed on the trees, walked through the rivers, frolicked in the woods. Life was good. Then one day the snake appeared and told them that they weren't really having fun because they weren't keeping score. Adam and Eve didn't understand the concept of keeping score, so the snake explained. "If you don't keep score you will never know who is best!"

It was changed after that. There was mucho yelling, and new rules had to be made continually for their games. There were always arguments about the rules and the points. God became angry when he found out that Adam and Eve were spending more time on rules than enjoying life. He confronted the two, but they just said they were having more fun keeping score and figuring out the rules.

God wouldn't listen- Adam and Eve were kicked out of the Garden and couldn't return until they stopped keeping score. Adam and Eve were stubborn, they felt that if they could raise their score above 20,000 before they died, and they would have known they accomplished something. They felt that without scoring there was no purpose to play.

After a year, God returned to Adam and Eve and asked them about their expulsion from the Garden.

"Well", said Adam. "The Garden was beautiful, the flowing rivers, the beautiful flowers and the fields. Life outside of the Garden is difficult. But, on the other hand, I now have 25,000 points! I am trying to hit 30,000 before I die." by Ann Herbert

So, how many points do you have?

Part of this is that our body is the only thing in the present! Our minds and our thoughts are either in the past (mistakes or things that were done to us) or in the future (fears and worries about what will be). If your mind gets mired in the past, it usually leads to some level of depression. If you get stuck in the future it can lead to some level of anxiety. We are caught my friends. **The good news is that there is a way out.** A way to change, a way to begin enjoying the present, rather than bemoaning the past and worrying about the future. The salvation (maybe too strong a word) is Mindfulness and Meditation.

Mindfulness

So, what is mindfulness? - we've all heard of the concept. Well mindfulness is opposite everything that we've learned growing up. It's slowing down, not speeding up, it's concentrating on one task, not multitasking, it's enjoying the moment, not considering the future, it's forgiving yourself and others, not being stuck in the muck and mire of past mistakes, anger and guilt.

I remember (a thousand years ago) when I was in graduate school, reading about eastern philosophy (I had to read the Tao- {translated as "The Way"}- many times before I could convince my New York City brain that it might make some sense), and how it was more important to give away, then to gain. That if you really want to gain, to have to give away, not collect more. I still have much trouble with this concept, as my upbringing constantly interferes with me. The whole concept is counter intuitive to me. In order to get you must give- it took me a while. It's still evolving.

So, mindfulness is learning how to enjoy the present. Learning how to turn on *the brake system*. It is the ability to stay in the moment, not think of the next task you have. So, while you're cleaning the kitchen, don't think about cleaning the bathroom. Stay in the kitchen!

A test: every time you stop at a red light- for one day- take a cleansing breath (breathe in through your nose and push your stomach out- hold for a beat and out slowly through your mouth, pulling your stomach in). Can you do that for one full day? Not missing one light- not forgetting it once? If you can I salute you!

In this tiny guide- I am only going to introduce you to these concepts.

Sign up here for my free webinar:
https://www.livingemotionalintelligence.com/webinar/

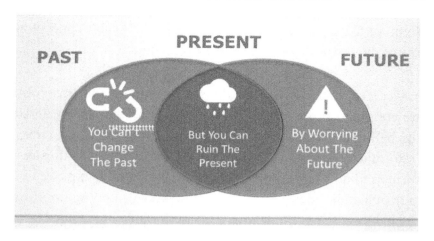

Meditation

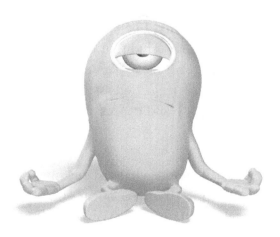

I have found that meditation is a very scary word for people. There are many myths about meditation which seems to worry people, such as: it's religious (and therefore I shouldn't do because it goes against my faith); and you need to have a guru to learn the technique. There are many untruths about meditation.

Some of the worst are: "I don't have time", "I can't concentrate as it is, how will I be able to learn to meditate."

In fact, every religion uses meditative techniques and most forms are not spiritual nor religious. You betray no one, nor invalidate any belief, by learning meditation (other than your toxic stress). Unfortunately, we have become comfortable in our toxic stress. We don't know any better. We've done it for so long, we're used to it (remember our self-destructive patterns). Letting go of our bad habits is scary. Somehow, I'm comfortable being nuts!

We in the West are especially good at resisting meditation. In Buddhist literature they speak of the *five hindrances* that interfere with our ability to meditate (these are mental games we use to avoid meditation- in actuality, I believe that there are many more than five.) In the Eastern Tradition the five hindrances are: *sensory desire* (our need to experience things through our external senses); *ill will* (rejection of the concept); *sloth and torpor* (heaviness of body and depression); *restlessness/ worry*; and *doubt.*

But let's look at our culture- what are our hindrances? How do we resist meditation? First, we have a fear of it- it is strange to us- therefore we doubt it (East bad, West good)- and we doubt whether we can do it. Our minds you see, are active and used to moving- meditation is asking us to slow that process down. So therefore, we take the approach of "It sounds good, but not for me!" "I don't have time for this silliness- I am a busy person". Second, many of us don't like even closing our eyes. When we close our eyes, it means it's time for sleep. We have a fear of letting go- it might lead to us not being in control. If you really want fear, there is a stance in Tai Chi called Whu Chi (the state of nothingness). Unfortunately, many of us do not learn discipline. And make no mistake, meditation is a discipline.

Meditation is a simple thing, that is very difficult to maintain. It has to become part of your routine like anything else. In fact, the way you develop a habit is doing it at least 21 times. That's 21 days before it becomes part of you.

Meditation is hard to start. When you close your eyes your mind immediately wanders to other subjects. It's like paper training a dog. You put them on the paper and they run off. So, you bring them back, and they run off. Eventually hopefully your determination will prevail. So that's what your mind is like, a hyperactive little dog, running with little direction and at times, little purpose (it's cute in puppies, not cute in people).

So, what is meditation. Meditation is learning how to slow down and stop your racing mind. It is a *Mind Vacation.* It reverses the destruction of Toxic Stress. It is centering your body and thoughts in the present, and for a few glorious moments, not worrying about anything, but being. But I will warn you, it will become addictive!

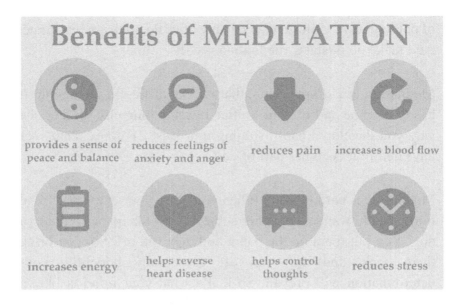

In the free webinar you will learn a brief meditation. Yes, by the end of the webinar you will be meditating. A couple of Apps to help: Buddhify- Headspace and Calm.

Power Down

First some scary statistics (from infographics)

- The average person checks their cellphone 110 times per day

- 1 in 5 people have used their smartphones during sex.

- 12% of people use the cellphones in the shower

- 50% of teens will admit addiction to it

- Cellphone use responsible for 26% of car accidents

- 75% of people admit to texting while driving

- 56% of people check their devices during driving.

Is it possible- Is it possible to live without our cell phones or the internet? I think not! We are too far gone- It has replaced or at best, redefined friendships and social relationships in adolescence. So, since we can't move backwards with technology, we have to learn to control and modify.

Take a deep breath and turn off your phone- leave it off for an hour. See if you last!

Don't take your phone to restaurants- leave it in the car. Talk to people rather than to electronics. (yeah but my pictures- what if someone wants to contact me) I think you'll be ok after a hour or two- the world won't come crashing down. Take a chance!

Family rule- no cell phones at the table

Sleep

One last issue before moving on. That is our need for **restoration**- our need for sleep. Lack of adequate rest has tremendous impacts on our system. And these impacts are not just being tired.

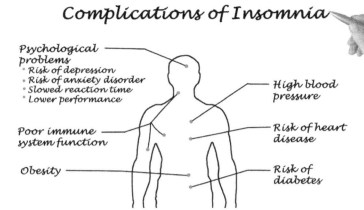

Complications of Insomnia

Psychological problems
- Risk of depression
- Risk of anxiety disorder
- Slowed reaction time
- Lower performance

High blood pressure

Poor immune system function

Risk of heart disease

Obesity

Risk of diabetes

I don't want to belabor this point, but tiredness has been called "**The Performance Killer**"

Next Steps

I hope you learned some things- Of course in such a short book it's hard to cover everything- but I hope you get the idea.

So what is your next step?

Watch the FREE Webinar - Here is a link:

https://www.livingemotionalintelligence.com/webinar/

Livingemotionalintelligence.com

In the Webinar, you will learn three important techniques:

A top down technique- asking certain questions about worries and problems

&

A meditative technique to turn the brake system on

&

And some simple rules for getting better sleep.

After that, you can sign up for my Master Class- and get a deeper understanding of your own and others emotions and reactions.

The class is centered on how to improve your emotional intelligence. It consists of over 30 videos- learning about yourself and others and improving top down awareness and control. It also includes the next steps in meditation.

Here is the link for the Master Class:

https://www.livingemotionalintelligence.com/master-class/

This is Dr. Jeffrey Donner- The Sultan of Psychology- wishing everyone a:

pleasant present.

P.S. Oh yes- one other thing (almost forgot) If you have interest in psychological thrillers or historical fiction- check out my other website:

www.jeffdonner.com

You can also sign up for a free newsletter on that site!

Made in the USA
Coppell, TX
22 January 2021

48640305R10046